**Dear Parents,**

Welcome to the Magic School Bus!

For over 20 years, teachers, parents, and children have been enchanted and inspired by Ms. Frizzle and the fabulous cast of beloved characters that make up The Magic School Bus series.

The unusual field trips, visual jokes, eye-catching details, and interesting information are just a few of the elements that make The Magic School Bus series an excellent tool to get your child excited about school, reading, and exploring their world.

It is important that children learn to read well enough to succeed in school and beyond. Here are some ideas for reading this book with your child:

- Look at the book together. Encourage your child to read the title and make a prediction about the story.
- Read the book together. Encourage your child to sound out words when appropriate. When your child struggles, you can help by providing the word.
- Encourage your child to retell the story. This is a great way to check for comprehension.

Enjoy the experience of helping your child learn to read and love to read!

Visit www.scholastic.com/magicschoolbus to subscribe to Scholastic's free parent e-newsletter, and find book lists, read-aloud tips, and learning hints for pre-readers, beginners, and older kids, too. Inspire a love of books in your child!

There are many Magic School Bus books for your reader to enjoy. We think you will enjoy these, too:

Ms. Frizzle

Mr. Bones

Liz

Written by Kristin Earhart
Illustrated by Carolyn Bracken

Based on The Magic School Bus® books
Written by Joanna Cole and illustrated by Bruce Degen

The author and editor would like to thank Stephen C. Allen, MD,
for his expert advice in preparing the manuscript and illustrations.

ISBN 978-0-545-23950-9

12 11 10 9 8 7 6                                    14 15/0

First printing, October 2010                 40
Printed in the U.S.A.

Designed by Rick DeMonico

# The Magic School Bus®
## Fixes a Bone

Arnold    Ralphie    Keesha    Phoebe    Carlos    Tim    Wanda    Dorothy Ann

Cartwheel
·B·O·O·K·S·®

## SCHOLASTIC INC.

New York    Toronto    London    Auckland
Sydney    Mexico City    New Delhi    Hong Kong

It's fun to be in Ms. Frizzle's class.
Sometimes we go on trips
in the Magic School Bus.

4

But today we are having a Halloween party.
We will have a good time.

OUR LESSONS WILL BE SPOOKY, TOO.

"Time to learn about bones," says Ms. Frizzle.

"What about our room?" Tim asks.

"We want it to be scary," D.A. adds.

"Do you think skeletons are scary?" asks the Friz.

Ms. Frizzle points to our skeleton.
"We can learn a lot from Mr. Bones," she says.

7

Carlos pins a spider to the wall.

He rushes to his seat.

Uh-oh! Carlos does not watch where he is going.

Poor Mr. Bones!

Mr. Bones gets up all by himself.
He is amazing!

CLASS, MR. BONES IS VERY SPECIAL.

THANK YOU, MS. FRIZZLE.

DIFFERENT SHAPE, DIFFERENT JOB

by Wanda

Your bones have different jobs, so they come in different shapes.

- The skull gives the head its shape.

- The spine can twist (side to side) and bend (up and down).

- The ribs protect the heart and lungs.

Our class skeleton can talk!
"Are you okay, Mr. Bones?" Ms. Frizzle asks.
Carlos looks worried.

I THINK I BROKE MY HUMERUS.

HE THINKS IT'S HUMOROUS?
A BROKEN BONE ISN'T FUNNY!

THIS IS THE HUMERUS.
SAY: **HEW**-MUH-RUSS.

"We have to help him," Carlos declares.

"To the bus, class!" calls the Friz.

"You rest here, Mr. Bones. We'll be right back."

We climb on the bus.
It starts to shrink.
We get smaller and smaller.
We whiz back into the classroom.

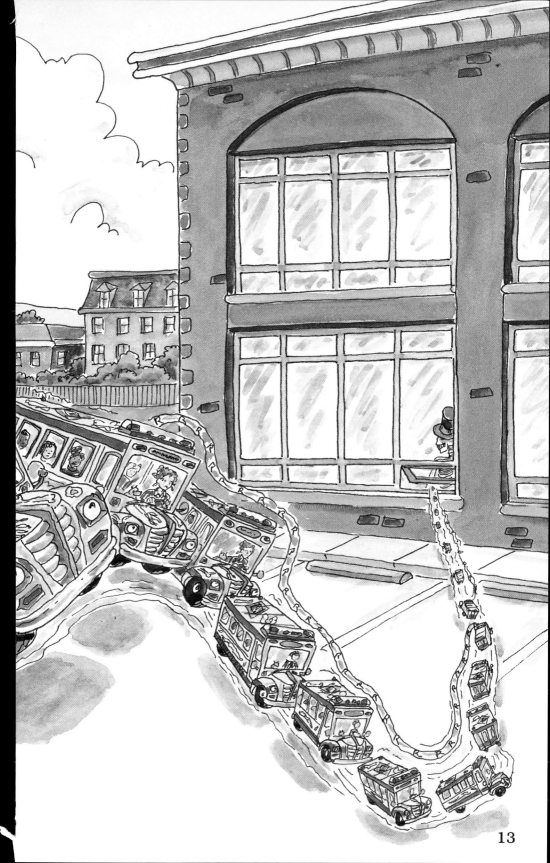

We fly toward Mr. Bones.
Then we fly *into* Mr. Bones.
"A lot happens in your bones,"
says the Friz.

14

We are small, so we can walk inside the bone.

"Our bones are strong," the Friz says.

"But they are also light."

THE OUTSIDE OF THE BONE IS VERY HARD.

BONE PARTS
by D.A.

Bones have parts.
The outside layer is very thin.
The next layer is hard and strong. It does not bend.
The inside layer is spongy.

OUTSIDE LAYER

SPONGY LAYER

INSIDE LAYER

17

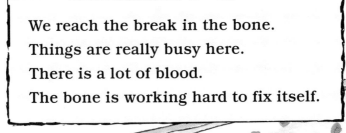

We reach the break in the bone.
Things are really busy here.
There is a lot of blood.
The bone is working hard to fix itself.

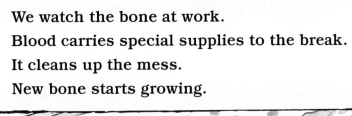

We watch the bone at work.
Blood carries special supplies to the break.
It cleans up the mess.
New bone starts growing.

ON THE MEND
by Arnold

Your bone heals itself in stages:
1) Blood covers the break.
2) The blood gets thick and holds the bone together.
3) New bone starts to grow.
4) The new bone makes a bridge between the broken pieces.

It might not be magic, but it is amazing!

"Mr. Bones needs a cast," Keesha says.

D.A. reads from her book.

"A cast is like a hard bandage," she says.

A CAST WILL HOLD THE BONE IN PLACE.

THEN IT CAN GROW BACK INTO ONE PIECE.

"Back on the bus," the Friz calls.
"We have a lot to do."

The bus zips out of Mr. Bones.
It zooms around his broken arm.
It wraps a cast around the bone.
Our work is done.

STEP BY STEP
by Carlos

If you break a bone, this is what happens:
Step 1: The doctor takes an X-ray—a special picture that shows how the bone is broken.

24

25

Now the bus is back in the parking lot.
We go back to our classroom.
We hang up more spooky stuff.

WE'RE BACK TO OUR NORMAL SIZE.

Carlos wheels Mr. Bones back to his spot.
He's glad the skeleton is getting better.
We all get to write on his cast.

29

31

# How to Have Healthy Bones

Strong bones are less likely to break.
Here are some tips for building strong bones:

- Eat foods like milk, yogurt, cheese, and leafy greens. They are high in calcium and magnesium, which are building blocks for bones.

- Spend time outside. Sunshine gives you Vitamin D, which helps your body use calcium.

- Get lots of exercise. Running and jumping around keep your bones strong.

- Always wear a helmet and other protective gear when bike riding or playing other sports to help prevent breaks.

**Q: Why didn't the skeleton cross the road?**

**A: He didn't have the guts!**